# Reading Essentials®
## in Social Studies

### COUNTRY CONNECTIONS

# SOUTH AFRICA

#### JOANNE MATTERN

Perfection Learning®

Editorial Director: Susan C. Thies

Editor: Mary L. Bush

Cover Design: Michael A. Aspengren

Inside Design: Michelle J. Glass

**IMAGE CREDITS:** ©Charles O'Rear/CORBIS: pp. 6, 9, 28–29; ©Nik Wheeler/CORBIS: p. 7; ©Darrell Gulin/CORBIS: p. 14; ©Charles & Josette Lenars/CORBIS: p. 21; ©Bettmann/CORBIS: p. 23; ©David & Peter Tumley/CORBIS: pp. 24, 32–33; ©Bob Krist/CORBIS: p. 26; ©Nicole Duplaix/CORBIS: p. 33; ©Nubar Alexanian/CORBIS: pp. 38–39

ArtToday (www.arttoday.com): pp. 12, 13, 35 (right), 37, 42, 43, 44; Corbis: back cover, pp. 5, 18 (left), 19; Corel Professional Photos: front cover, pp. 1, 10–11 (background), 11, 15, 16, 17, 18 (top & bottom), 20, 24–25 (middle), 30, 30–31 (background), 34 (left & bottom), 34–35 (middle), 41; MapArt: pp. 4, 10, 14, 31

# TABLE OF CONTENTS

# Just the FACTS!

**Location** South Africa is located at the southern tip of Africa. The Atlantic Ocean lies to South Africa's west, while the Indian Ocean lies to its east. Four African countries border South Africa—Namibia, Botswana, Zimbabwe, and Mozambique.

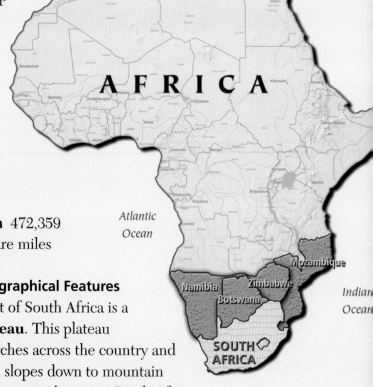

AFRICA

Atlantic Ocean

Mozambique

Namibia    Zimbabwe

Botswana    Indian Ocean

SOUTH AFRICA

**Area** 472,359 square miles

> **HOW BIG IS THAT?**
>
> South Africa covers a larger area than California, Arizona, Utah, and Nevada combined.

**Geographical Features** Most of South Africa is a **plateau**. This plateau stretches across the country and then slopes down to mountain ranges near the coast. South Africa also has **deserts** and **rain forests**.

**Highest Elevation**  Champagne Castle Mountain
(3,375 feet above sea level)

**Lowest Elevation**  Atlantic Ocean coastline
(sea level)

**Climate**  Most of South Africa has a **temperate
climate**. The deserts, however, experience long periods
of hot, dry weather, and the eastern coast often has a
hot, **humid** climate.

**Capital City**  South Africa has three capitals. Pretoria is
the **executive** capital and the seat of the government.
Cape Town is the **legislative** capital. Bloemfontein is
the **judicial** capital.

**Largest Cities**  Cape Town, Johannesburg, Pretoria,
Durban

**Population**  43,486,097 (2001)

**Languages**  Xhosa, Zulu, Tswana, Swazi, Afrikaans,
English

**Main Religion**  Christianity

**Government**  South Africa is a **republic**. The president is the head of the government. South Africa is divided into nine **provinces**.

**CAN YOU NAME THEM?**

South Africa's provinces are Eastern Cape, Free State, Gauteng, KwaZulu-Natal, Mpumalanga, North West, Northern Cape, Northern Province, and Western Cape.

**Industries**  mining, automobile assembly, metalworking, machinery, textiles, iron and steel production, chemicals, fertilizer, food products

**Natural Resources**
gold, platinum, chromium, coal, iron ore, diamonds, copper, natural gas, corn, wheat, sugarcane, fruits, vegetables, beef, poultry, dairy products

**Currency**  basic unit is the rand

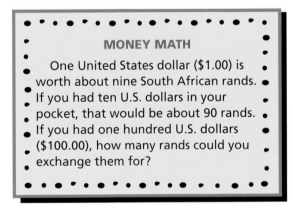

**MONEY MATH**

One United States dollar ($1.00) is worth about nine South African rands. If you had ten U.S. dollars in your pocket, that would be about 90 rands. If you had one hundred U.S. dollars ($100.00), how many rands could you exchange them for?

**South African rands**

**FLAG OF MANY COLORS**

In 1994, South Africa marked the end of **apartheid** and the election of its first black president with a new flag. This flag was designed to represent the country's unity.

## CHAPTER 1

# Beneath Your Feet

## South Africa's Land and Climate

Located in southern Africa, South Africa's 472,359 square miles of land stretch across plateaus, mountains, deserts, and coastal plains.

## GEOGRAPHICAL FEATURES

Most of central South Africa is part of the Plateau region. The largest area within this region is called the High Veld. The High Veld is 4,000 to 6,000 feet high and covered by grasslands.

In the midst of the Plateau is a mountain range called the Witwatersrand Ridge. The Witwatersrand has many rich gold deposits.

South Africa also has many other mountains. The Great Escarpment is made up of several mountain ranges that line the southern and eastern edges of the Plateau. The Great Escarpment includes the Drakensberg mountain range. This is the highest mountain range in southern Africa and includes Champagne Castle Mountain, the highest point in South Africa.

> **WATER, ANYONE?**
>
> *Karroo* means "land of thirst" in the language of the African Bushmen.

Table Mountain

The Cape Mountains rise in the southern end of the country. Between these mountains and the Great Escarpment lie two very dry, hot plateaus—the Great Karroo and the Little Karroo. Few people live in this part of the country because of its climate.

Two large deserts cover areas of South Africa. The Namib Desert lies along the Atlantic Ocean above the Cape Mountains. The Kalahari Desert stretches across the northern edge of the Plateau. The Kalahari extends into the neighboring country of Botswana.

South Africa has 2,700 miles of coast along the Atlantic and Indian Oceans. Most of this land is hilly.

**TABLE TALK**

Table Mountain is a popular tourist attraction in South Africa. This mountain is located near the city of Cape Town. It rises 3,563 above sea level, and the top is often covered by thick white clouds. This mountain got its name because its top is flat like a table. The clouds that cover the top are called "the mountain's tablecloth."

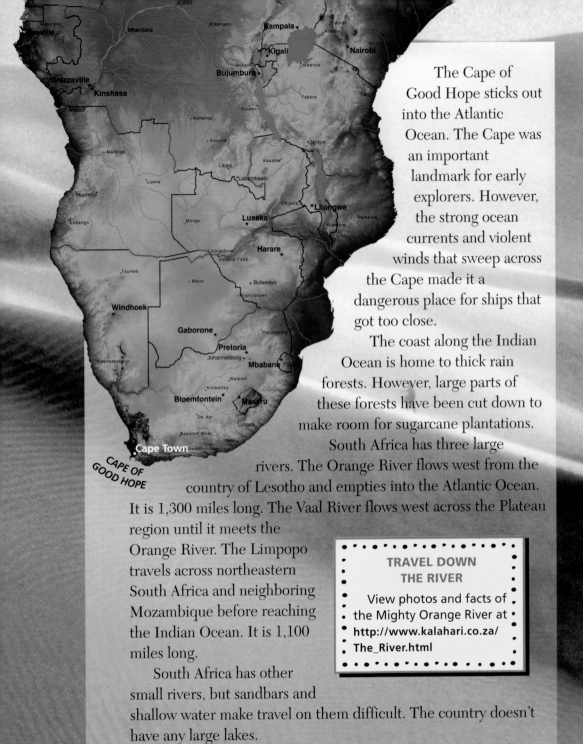

The Cape of Good Hope sticks out into the Atlantic Ocean. The Cape was an important landmark for early explorers. However, the strong ocean currents and violent winds that sweep across the Cape made it a dangerous place for ships that got too close.

The coast along the Indian Ocean is home to thick rain forests. However, large parts of these forests have been cut down to make room for sugarcane plantations.

South Africa has three large rivers. The Orange River flows west from the country of Lesotho and empties into the Atlantic Ocean. It is 1,300 miles long. The Vaal River flows west across the Plateau region until it meets the Orange River. The Limpopo travels across northeastern South Africa and neighboring Mozambique before reaching the Indian Ocean. It is 1,100 miles long.

South Africa has other small rivers, but sandbars and shallow water make travel on them difficult. The country doesn't have any large lakes.

TRAVEL DOWN
THE RIVER

View photos and facts of the Mighty Orange River at http://www.kalahari.co.za/ The_River.html

## THE CLIMATE

Most of South Africa has a mild climate. It's sunny and warm in the summer and colder in the winter.

But some of the more extreme regions, such as the deserts, mountaintops, and coastal regions, have varying weather. The deserts are hot and dry much of the year. Some high mountains are covered with snow all year long. Meanwhile, the northeastern coast, where the rain forests grow, has a **tropical** climate.

Rainfall is also different across the country. The eastern coast usually receives more rain than the west, where the desert regions are located. Most of the country receives less than 25 inches of rain a year.

## CHAPTER 2

# Living Wonders

## The Plants and Animals of South Afric

Although it is a small country, South Africa is home to many different animals and plants. Most of South Africa's wildlife is **native** to the country. The remaining plants and animals were brought to South Africa from other parts of the world.

### PLANTS

About 22,000 species, or types, of plants are found in South Africa. Most of these plants are grasses and shrubs that grow best in the country's grasslands and **savannas**. Grasslands cover eastern central South Africa, while the savanna is found in the north and northeastern area of the country. The savanna has long grasses, along with baobab and mopani trees. Some parts of these regions are so dry most of the year that only short grasses and scrubby plants can survive. When rain falls in the spring, however, colorful wildflowers decorate the land.

> **PLANTS, PLANTS, AND MORE PLANTS!**
>
> Although South Africa is much smaller than the United States or Russia, it has more plant species than either of those larger countries.

Baobab trees thrive in dry areas and cannot survive flooding.

**TREE OF LIFE**

The baobab is a gigantic tree with a long history in Africa. For details and a picture of this unique tree, go to http://www.naturelink.co.za/ Descriptions/Baobab.htm.

South Africa has few forests. In fact, only 1 percent of Africa's land is forestland. The majority of this land is found along the coasts of the western and eastern Cape. Most of these forests are filled with **hardwood** trees, such as lemonwood and ironwood. **Conifers**, such as pine trees, can also be found in wooded areas. These trees were brought to South Africa from Europe and North America in order to provide timber and wood pulp.

The Great Karroo is covered with plants that can survive the heat and dryness. Some of the plants that grow there have life cycles that are geared to the occasional storms that pass through the region.

Proteas

**FLOWER MYTHS**

Proteas grow in many different shapes, sizes, and colors. Because of this, they were named after the Greek god Proteus. According to mythology, Proteus was able to change his appearance whenever he wanted.

The Fynbos **biome** is a special plant community located in the southern Cape. It is one of the world's six Floral Kingdoms and is the only one contained in just one country. More than 8,500 different species of plants grow in the Fynbos biome. Many of these plants cannot be found anywhere else in the world. One of these plants is the protea, an evergreen shrub that is South Africa's national flower. The protea has spiky flower heads that can grow as large as a foot wide.

↖ Fynbos biome

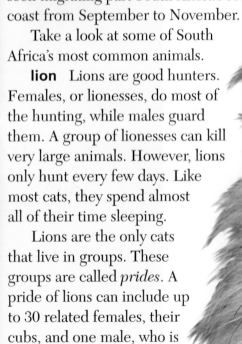

**NAME THAT WHALE**

Southern right whales can be found swimming along South Africa's coast in the spring. After having their babies, they return to Antarctica for the rest of the year.

The Southern right whale got its name because it lived in the Southern Hemisphere and was the "right" whale to kill because it swims very slowly and floats when harpooned. Now, however, there are laws protecting this whale from becoming endangered.

# ANIMALS

South Africa has a huge variety of animals. Long ago, these animals roamed throughout the country. Today, most of them are found in game parks or wildlife preserves.

Hundreds of bird species fly through South Africa's skies, as well as walk the land. Eagles, falcons, hawks, and vultures circle the country's mountains. In the grassland and savanna regions, orioles, rollers, bishop birds, loeries, and hoopoes swoop across the plains. Spoonbills, herons, cranes, storks, and pelicans live near rivers and ocean shorelines.

In addition, 39 different species of whales can be seen migrating past South Africa's southern coast from September to November.

Take a look at some of South Africa's most common animals.

**lion** Lions are good hunters. Females, or lionesses, do most of the hunting, while males guard them. A group of lionesses can kill very large animals. However, lions only hunt every few days. Like most cats, they spend almost all of their time sleeping.

Lions are the only cats that live in groups. These groups are called *prides*. A pride of lions can include up to 30 related females, their cubs, and one male, who is the pride's leader.

**leopard**  A leopard can be as long as 8 feet from nose to tail. It hunts at night and uses its excellent senses of sight and hearing to help find its **prey**. Once the leopard locates its prey, it creeps up on it slowly and quietly. Then it charges forward and attacks. Leopards also leap down from trees to attack their prey.

The leopard is an expert tree climber. These cats spend most of their time in trees. Besides sleeping there, they drag their prey up into the trees to keep it safe from hyenas and other animals. A leopard's prey includes large animals, such as antelope and monkeys.

**elephant**  The African bush elephant is the largest land mammal alive today. The biggest one ever found weighed about $13\frac{1}{2}$ tons. An elephant's skin alone weighs about a ton!

Because it's so large, the elephant needs a lot of food. An African elephant spends up to 16 hours a day searching for leaves and plants to eat. These elephants are strong enough to push over trees to reach the leaves on the top branches.

The most interesting feature of an elephant is its trunk. Small fingerlike bumps on the end of the trunk can pick up objects as small as berries. Elephants communicate by

> **LOOK OUT FOR THE ELEPHANTS!**
>
> South Africa has the largest elephant herd in the world. The herd is found in a safari park in Maputaland, KwaZula-Natal. It has more than 150 members.

making loud trumpeting noises and other sounds through their trunks. They also use their trunks to spray water over themselves to cool off.

**hippopotamus**  This big, heavy animal is related to the pig. Hippos spend most of the day resting in lakes. This animal is so heavy, it is more comfortable in the water than it is on land. Water helps support the hippo's huge body. It also keeps the hippo cool and moist. If a hippo's skin gets too dry, it will die. A hippo can stay underwater for up to six minutes.

Hippos feed at night. They eat grass and water plants using their lips and sharp teeth like lawnmowers to pull up the food. A hippo can eat up to 180 pounds of plant material in one night.

**rhinoceros**  There are two types of African rhinoceroses—the black rhino and the white rhino. Despite their names, both rhinos are actually gray.

The black rhinoceros's upper lip is shaped like a hook. It lets the rhino pull leaves and twigs from plants. A black rhino also stands on its back legs and breaks off tree branches with its horn. It can even eat the sharp thorns on an acacia tree because its mouth is so tough.

Black rhinos are about 12 feet long and weigh up to 2,300 pounds. They can run as fast as 30 miles per hour over short distances.

A white rhino's mouth is shaped differently than a black rhino's. That's because it eats different food. Instead of pulling leaves and twigs from trees, the white rhino grazes on short grass.

Rhinos don't have sweat glands. They bathe in water or roll in mud to cool off.

Although rhinos have very bad eyesight, they have a fantastic sense of smell. This helps them find food and avoid **predators**, such as lions.

**zebra**  Zebras usually live in small family groups, but they combine to form larger herds during the dry season. Zebras will even roam the savanna with antelopes and wildebeests. Each herd is led by a male zebra, or stallion. These stallions can be very fierce. They often kick at enemies with their sharp hooves. A kick from a zebra can break an animal's jaw or teeth.

A zebra's stripes help it hide from its enemies. As zebras move in and out of the shadows of the long grass, their stripes make them hard to see. Stripes also help zebras identify one another. Every zebra has its own unique pattern of stripes.

**springbok** The springbok is a small member of the antelope family. It can leap very high and far. Like other

Springbok

antelope, the springbok lives in large herds. It grazes on savanna grasses.

**wildebeest** The wildebeest is another type of antelope. These animals gather in huge herds with thousands of members when they are **migrating**. They also travel with zebras and other antelopes. Wildebeests travel thousands of miles across the savanna in search of fresh grass to eat. Even baby wildebeests can run just a few hours after they're born.

**giraffe** The giraffe is the tallest animal on Earth. A full-grown giraffe can be 18 feet tall. Even a newborn giraffe is 6 feet tall! The giraffe's long neck lets it eat leaves high in the trees. This means it can find food in places other animals can't reach.

Herds of wildebeests, zebras, and elephants often travel with giraffes. That's because giraffes have excellent eyesight. They can spot food, water, and danger from far away.

Giraffes can run up to 35 miles per hour and leap 6-foot-tall fences. They will also kick fiercely with their sharp hooves when in danger.

**spotted hyena** Hyenas are both hunters and **scavengers**. These animals come out at night to hunt in groups. A hyena is only about 5 feet long and 3 feet high at the shoulder. But a group of hyenas can kill a much bigger animal, such as a wildebeest or zebra. The hyena's heavy jaws and powerful teeth are strong enough to crush bones. Hyenas also eat the remains of animals killed by others. These little animals are so fierce that a group of them can chase lions away from their kill.

Hyenas are famous for their laugh. But this animal isn't really laughing. When the hyena is excited or angry, it makes a high, shrill cry that sounds like a laugh.

**jackal** The jackal is a member of the dog family. But it isn't a hunter like a wild dog. Instead, it's a scavenger. Jackals will wait while larger animals kill and eat their prey. When the larger animals are finished, the jackals eat what's left. Jackals also find scraps of meat, vegetables, and other leftovers around people's houses.

Spotted hyena

**baboon** This member of the monkey family lives in large groups called *troops*. As many as 300 baboons make up a troop. They travel over the ground, looking for food. A baboon eats many different foods, including insects, worms, reptiles, small mammals, eggs, fruit, and plants.

There are many different types of baboons. The largest is the chacma of southern Africa. It is also called the pigtailed baboon. An adult male chacma can weigh up to 90 pounds.

Baboons are powerful, aggressive animals. But they also like to play. One baboon might jump on another's back for a piggyback ride! Baboons are also very smart. They can distinguish colors. These animals communicate with one another through a number of different cries and calls.

**SOUTH AFRICAN SAFARI**

South Africa's largest game park is Kruger National Park. This park is 50 miles wide and 200 miles long. It holds about 7,500 elephants and 2,000 lions. Go on a safari at Kruger National Park at this site.

http://www.krugersafari.com

**ostrich** The ostrich is the world's largest bird. Males can be up to 9 feet tall and weigh 345 pounds. In fact, this bird is so big, it can't fly! Its wings simply aren't strong enough to lift it off the ground. But that doesn't mean that an ostrich has trouble getting around. This bird is a great runner. Its long legs help it run up to 45 miles an hour. That's as fast as a racehorse!

The ostrich also lays the world's largest eggs. An ostrich egg is about 6–8 inches long, 4–6 inches around, and weighs close to 4 pounds. Africa's native people sometimes use ostrich eggs for food.

Because ostriches are so big and fast, they have few enemies. Even lions stay away from them because they can kick very hard.

Most of South Africa's wild animals live on wildlife preserves or in game parks. Many of these parks are found in the eastern part of the country. Game parks are like giant drive-through safaris. Visitors drive through the parks and watch animals from their cars. The animals in the game parks are cared for by specially trained wildlife managers called *rangers*. These rangers protect the animals and make sure they stay healthy. Their efforts have saved some animals, such as the rhinoceros, from becoming extinct.

## CHAPTER 3

# Looking Back South Africa's History

## SOUTH AFRICA'S FIRST PEOPLE

Scientists think that the human race may have begun in South Africa. They have found evidence that humanlike creatures lived in southern Africa two to three million years ago.

About 200,000 years ago, hunter-gatherers lived in South Africa. These **nomads** used fire and built simple shelters as they wandered around the country, hunting animals and gathering plants for food. About 15,000 years ago, these people divided into two different cultures. The San people continued to live as hunter-gatherers. The Khoikhoi, or Khoi, settled in one place and herded sheep. Both of these groups were small, slender, and had light brown skin.

Later, taller people with darker skin came to South Africa from the central part of the continent. These people were called the Bantu. The Bantu are the **ancestors** of today's black South Africans. This tribe conquered the San and Khoi. They brought cattle herding, mining, and farming to South Africa. They also founded large empires ruled by kings and priests.

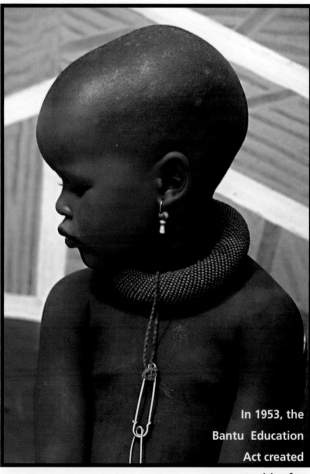

In 1953, the Bantu Education Act created opportunities for Bantu children to attend better schools.

# THE EUROPEANS ARRIVE

During the 1400s, explorers from Portugal sailed around the tip of Africa on their way to the East Indies. Many stopped at the Cape of Good Hope, where they met the Bantu. Later, explorers from the Dutch East India Company in the Netherlands, along with English explorers, also traveled along this trade route and had contact with South Africa's native people.

In 1647, a group of Dutch sailors were shipwrecked on the Cape of Good Hope. After they were rescued, they urged the Dutch East India Company to set up a supply station at the Cape. This settlement was built in 1652 and became a Dutch **colony** known as Cape Town.

Fifteen thousand white people lived in Cape Town by 1775. Most were Dutch, but others were German and French. These people became known as Afrikaners. They spoke a language called Afrikaans, which was based on the Dutch language. The Afrikaners followed a strict religion. This religion taught that different races should live separately and the white race should rule other races.

Some Afrikaners settled in the countryside about 400 miles north of Cape Town. They were called Boers. The Boers herded sheep and cattle. They took a lot of land away from the Khoi and San people. Most of these native South Africans were forced to move to the desert. Many others died from disease or battles with the Boers.

> **DUTCH FARMERS**
>
> *Boer* is the Dutch word for "farmer."

# TORN APART BY WAR

The Boers continued to move north and east. By 1779, they had run into Bantu settlements. From 1779 to 1781, the two groups fought a series of battles. Although the Bantu won several battles, the Boers had guns that ultimately helped them defeat the natives.

The Boers also fought with the British. Great Britain captured the Cape in 1806 during Britain's war against the Netherlands. In 1814, a peace treaty confirmed that South Africa was a British colony.

The Boers hadn't liked being ruled by the Dutch East India Company. But they didn't want the British to tell them what to do either. Many Boers traveled deep into the colony to get away from

British control. This journey became known as the Great Trek. By the early 1850s, the Boers had created two independent republics—the Transvaal and the Orange Free State.

Soon after the Boer republics were founded, gold and diamonds were discovered there. The British wanted to take over the republics so they could mine these new riches. Between 1899 and 1902, the British and the Boers fought the Anglo-Boer War. The war ended with a British victory.

In 1910, the Orange Free State and the Transvaal joined two British colonies—the Cape and Natal—to form the Union of South Africa. Although South Africa was part of the British Empire, it was allowed to rule itself.

## A NATION DIVIDED

South Africa was a nation of segregation, or separation. There were four groups of people in the country, each of which remained separate from the others. Huge differences in quality of life and human rights existed between the groups.

The white people ruled the country. The majority of these people were of Dutch, German, and French **descent**. Others came from Great Britain. They had most of the money and good jobs.

Civil Rights heroine Rosa Parks opposes apartheid outside the South African Embassy in Washington.

The three remaining groups didn't enjoy the same high quality of life. The black people, or Africans, worked for low pay at difficult jobs in mines and factories or on farms. People of mixed black, white, and Asian ancestry were known as coloreds. Coloreds also had fewer opportunities than whites. Asians, most of whom came from India, were considered a lower class as well.

In 1948, strict laws were passed to keep different races from living or working together. This system was called *apartheid*. Apartheid laws said that black people could only live in certain places. Many black families were forced to move to "homelands," which were poor, overcrowded areas with harsh living conditions. Blacks had their own schools, hospitals, transportation, and beaches. They had to carry a special Pass Book to identify themselves, their home address, and their job. Anyone who wasn't white needed special permission to travel away from home. Only white people were allowed to vote and make important decisions.

> **KEEPING SOUTH AFRICANS APART**
> *Apartheid* is an Afrikaans word that means "apartness."

## ONE MAN'S STAND AGAINST APARTHEID

One of the most outspoken critics of apartheid was a black man named Nelson Mandela. In 1962, Mandela was sentenced to life in prison because of his actions against apartheid. He was sent to a special jail for political prisoners on Robben Island, five miles off the coast of Cape Town. Mandela remained in a tiny prison cell for 28 years.

Even though he had little contact with the rest of the world, Mandela's defiance became a symbol of apartheid's unfairness. In 1990, the South African government released Mandela from prison. Mandela later went on to win the 1993 Nobel Peace Prize. In 1994, Mandela was elected South Africa's first black president.

Anyone who protested against apartheid was arrested and sent to prison. Many were tortured or killed by government soldiers or the police. Others, including many children, were killed in **riots** and other violent demonstrations. Apartheid lasted for 45 years.

## THE END OF APARTHEID

By 1990, countries around the world had joined together to protest apartheid. Many countries refused to trade with South Africa. Corporations refused to do business with the country or build factories there. Musicians and other entertainers would not perform there, and South African athletes were banned from many competitions, including the Olympics.

At the same time, pressure was growing from all races within South Africa to end apartheid. The country's **economy** was suffering, and people were angry about living in a place where they had so little freedom. South Africa's government realized that the country was in danger of collapsing if apartheid didn't end.

South Africa's white leaders, including President F. W. de Klerk, met with black leaders, such as Nelson Mandela and Archbishop Desmond Tutu. Together, they worked out peaceful ways to end apartheid.

### POWERFUL LEADERS

Both F. W. de Klerk and Archbishop Desmond Tutu were important in the fight to end apartheid. For more information on these leaders, check out the following Web sites:

http://assu.stanford.edu/speakers/bios/deklerk.html (F. W. de Klerk)

http://www.nobel.se/peace/laureates/1984/tutu-bio.html (Desmond Tutu)

In April 1994, elections were held in South Africa. For the first time, people of all races could vote. Nearly 20 million people turned out to elect Nelson Mandela president. He was the first black person to hold this office in the country's history.

Along with its first black president, South Africa also created a new constitution. This important document provides equal rights for all citizens. The government also created a Truth and Reconciliation Commission to bring justice to people who were the victims of crimes under apartheid. Some people who had committed crimes were sent to jail or received other forms of punishment. The country slowly began to heal from the years of separation and injustice.

**FOUR FLAGS IN ONE**

Prior to the 1994 elections, South Africa had a different flag than it has today. The old flag was actually four flags in one. The flag's background was the orange, white, and blue flag of the Netherlands. In the center of the white stripe were three miniature flags—the British Union flag and two former Boer republic flags.

South Africa's flag prior to 1994

## CHAPTER 4

# Digging In to South Africa's Resources and Industries

## MINERALS

South Africa has some of the richest mineral deposits in the world. Two-thirds of South Africa's **exports** are minerals. Mining and the manufacturing of mineral products are major industries in South Africa.

The country is the world's largest supplier of platinum. Large amounts of coal, chromium, iron, copper, and uranium are also mined.

South Africa also produces 40 percent of all the gold in the world and 20 percent of the world's diamonds. At first, gold and diamonds were extracted from pit mines, which were large holes dug in the ground. Pit mines can be used when the minerals are close to the surface. However, deeper **resources** cannot be removed from the earth this way. To reach them, miners have to work in deep shafts far under the ground. These working conditions make mining hard, dirty, and dangerous work. On average, one miner is killed for every ton of gold produced.

### PLATINUM PROVINCES

Platinum is a precious grayish white metal often used to make jewelry. The Northern and North West Provinces are sometimes called the "Platinum Provinces" because of their many platinum mines.

### PRECIOUS DISCOVERIES

Diamonds were first discovered in 1867 near the Orange River. Gold was first discovered in the eastern Transvaal in 1871.

Irrigation ditches with water wheels are one method of bringing water to South Africa's dry farmland.

## WATER

Because South Africa receives little rain, water is a scarce resource. Water shortages are common in many parts of the country, and water is often **rationed**. To solve this problem, several dams have been built and deep wells have been dug to tap into underground water reserves. **Irrigation** is also used to bring water to dry parts of the land.

## AGRICULTURE

Much of South Africa's land is used for ranching. The grasslands of the central plateau provide food for grazing cattle and sheep.

Farming is not a major industry in South Africa. It makes up only about five percent of the country's economy. Most of the country does not receive enough rain for successful farming, so only about 12 percent of the land is farmed. However, the few farms that South Africa has are very productive and provide enough food to feed the country's people.

South Africa's most important crop is maize, or corn. Wheat, sugarcane, and citrus fruits are also grown.

South Africa also harvests a large amount of grapes. These grapes are used to make wine. The country's vineyards are located near Cape Town. South Africa is the ninth-largest producer of wine in the world.

## INDUSTRIES

Johannesburg is the chief industrial center of South Africa. Here and in other South African cities, many people work in plants and factories. Major products manufactured include clothing, processed foods, chemicals, machinery, jewelry, and other **consumer goods**. Banking, trade, transportation, and utilities are important service industries in the country. Other South Africans work in business offices, schools, and hospitals.

**MOUNTAIN TEA**

Rooibos is a plant used to make a special tea. This plant is only found in the mountain regions of South Africa. For information about rooibos and its products, along with recipes, go to http://www.rooibosltd.co.za/index.htm.

**HEART HISTORY**

South Africa has an important place in medical history. In 1967, the first human heart transplant was performed at the Groote Schuur Hospital in Cape Town.

CHAPTER 5

# The Many Faces of South Africa

## Discovering South Africa's People

Decorat
beadwor
the center
tradition
Zulu clothi

# A LAND OF MANY CULTURES

Many different **ethnic** groups live in South Africa. Most of the population is black. They are members of African tribes such as the Zulu, Xhosa, and Sotho.

Another large ethnic group is the colored people. These people are a mix of black, white, and other races.

White residents are mostly descended from the country's early Dutch and British settlers. Others are descendants of Russian and European Jews who came to South Africa in the early 1900s searching for religious freedom.

About 1½ million Asians live in South Africa. Many of these people are descended from Indians who came to South Africa in the 1860s to work on sugarcane plantations. More recently, a number of immigrants from China have settled in South Africa.

**INDIAN COMMUNITY OF INTEREST**

Durban is a large city located on the eastern coast of South Africa. More than half the people who live in Durban are of Indian descent.

Durban

**A HELPING HAND**

Mahatma Gandhi, who helped India win independence from Great Britain, lived in South Africa from 1906–1914. During this time, he led a campaign to end racial discrimination against Indians in South Africa.

## LIVING IN THE CITIES

People of all races live in South Africa's **urban** areas. South Africa's cities are a lot like cities in Europe. Modern skyscrapers and office buildings are surrounded by narrow stone streets and large parks filled with flowers.

South African
township

   Most white people live in clean, modern houses or apartments in
South Africa's cities and suburbs. These families often have black
people working for them as maids, housekeepers, and yard workers.

   Many of South Africa's blacks live in poor communities on the
edges of cities. These communities are called *townships*. Township
houses are built from old pieces of wood and metal, sheets of plastic,
and pieces of cardboard or tin. Most of the streets aren't paved, and
there are no sewer systems or clean water supplies.

   During apartheid, townships were home to black families who
were forced to relocate from "white" neighborhoods. Today, townships
provide homes for workers who have moved into cities from the
country to find work. These blacks often work in the mines or
factories, as street vendors, or as domestic servants.

## LIVING IN THE COUNTRY

Some parts of **rural** South Africa still look like they did hundreds of years ago. Many rural families live in houses made of natural materials. Traditional Zulu houses, for example, are round huts made of grass. Other traditional homes, called *kraals*, are cone-shaped structures of dirt and straw.

Other rural areas are covered by ranches or farms. Large agricultural businesses are mostly owned by wealthy white families. These families use modern machinery, such as tractors and **combines**, to harvest crops. Black farmers and ranchers usually have small areas of poor-quality land. These farmers are not wealthy enough to use modern tools. Instead, they farm using simple tools and animals.

Kraals are arranged in circles to form a village.

33

## CHAPTER 6

# A Slice of Life

## South African Culture

## FOOD

Most South Africans eat **Western** food, such as sandwiches, hamburgers, and pizza. Families with European or Asian ancestors enjoy the foods of their homelands, such as curry (India), fish and chips (British), or pasta (Italy).

Traditional African foods are popular too. Corn is the most important food in South Africa. Most black people enjoy a corn and milk porridge called *mealie pap*.

Meat dishes are often the center of African cooking. Afrikaners enjoy barbecues, which are called *braaivleis*. A spicy sausage called *boerewors* is often eaten at barbecues. *Biltong*, or dried meat, is another tasty snack.

**lamb curry**

Biltong is often made from strips of deer meat. *Bobotie* is a curried meat loaf topped with an egg mixture. Spicy pork and lamb kabobs, called *sosaties*, are often the center of an African meal.

Corn is used in many South African dishes.

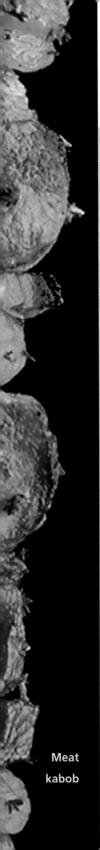

Because Afrikaners are descended from the Dutch, they have kept many Dutch cooking traditions. One popular Afrikaner dish is a type of apple pie called Dutch apple pudding. Here is the recipe.

# DUTCH APPLE PUDDING

## Ingredients

6 apples

2 tablespoons butter

1 cup +
3 tablespoons sugar

1 beaten egg

1 cup milk

2 cups sifted flour

1/4 teaspoon salt

3 teaspoons baking powder

1/2 teaspoon nutmeg

## Instructions

1. Preheat the oven to 325° F.

2. Ask an adult to peel and core the apples and cut them into quarters.

3. In a bowl, cream the butter, 1 cup of sugar, and the beaten egg. Add the milk, flour, salt, and baking powder.

4. Mix the batter into a soft dough, and spread it into a shallow baking dish.

5. Press the apple pieces into the dough.

6. Sprinkle the 3 tablespoons of sugar and the nutmeg over the top.

7. Bake for 45 to 60 minutes. Insert a knife into the center of your pudding. If it comes out clean, your pudding is ready to eat!

Meat
kabob

# EDUCATION

South African children must start school when they are six years old. They attend a primary school until the seventh grade. Then they go to high school for five years. After high school, some students attend universities to prepare for professional careers.

# LANGUAGE

Most business in South Africa is done in English. Two of South Africa's most common native languages are Zulu and Afrikaans. Practice saying some of these common expressions in both languages.

| English | Zulu | Afrikaans |
|---|---|---|
| hello | sabona (sah-BOH-nah) | hallo |
| How are you? | Sapele kunjani (sah-PEE-leh koon-JAN-nee) | Hoegaandit (hoo-CHAHND-it) |
| good-bye | sale kahle (salla KAHSH-leh) | totsiens (TOT-seens) |
| thank you | ngiyabonga (ni-gee-yah-BONG-ah) | dankie (DUNN-key) |
| please | ngiyancenga (ni-gee-yan-k-SENG-ah) | asseblief (us-ah-BLEEF) |

# SPORTS AND GAMES

South Africa's mild, dry climate is well suited for many outdoor activities. As is true of so much of South African life, different races participate in different sports.

Rugby (a British game that is like American football) is popular among whites and coloreds. So is the British sport of cricket. Cricket is a team sport in which players use a bat to try to "bowl" the ball through their opponent's **wicket**.

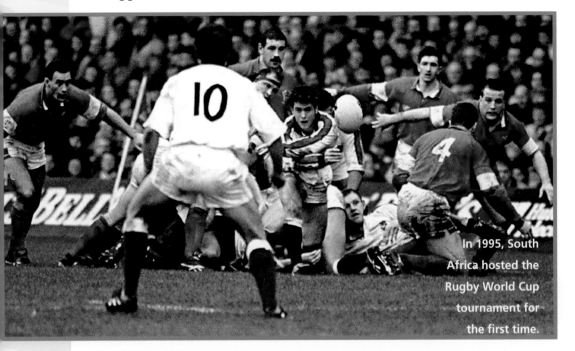

In 1995, South Africa hosted the Rugby World Cup tournament for the first time.

Soccer is one sport that is popular among both blacks and whites. South Africans are proud of their national team, which has won several major championships.

Because South Africa has miles of ocean coastline, swimming and sailing are popular pastimes. Beaches and swimming pools are usually crowded all year long.

Because of apartheid, South Africa did not compete in the Olympics from 1960 to 1992. During this time, some South African athletes moved to other countries to compete on their Olympic teams. Today, however, many South Africans participate in the Olympic Games representing their own country.

Board and card games are also popular in South Africa, especially among whites. Many whites play chess. Others enjoy a complicated card game called *bridge*. Many young people and families join leagues to play chess and bridge with others all over the country.

# HOLIDAYS

South Africans celebrate many national holidays. Some recognize important events in the struggle for equal rights. These celebrations include the Day of Reconciliation, Youth Day, Human Rights Day, and Freedom Day.

Along with national holidays, some parts of South Africa enjoy cultural festivals. The Roodepoort Eisteddfod takes place every other October in Roodepoort, a town in Gauteng province. It is the only international music, dance, and song festival in the Southern Hemisphere.

South Africans also enjoy the Grahamstown Festival on the Eastern Cape during July. During this festival, people attend concerts, plays, and street performances. Many famous South African performers first appeared at this festival.

On New Year's Day, hundreds of colored people dress up and sing and dance through Cape Town during the annual Coloreds' Carnival.

Other holidays celebrated in South Africa are religious. Christians celebrate Christmas on December 25. Like other Christians, many South Africans go to church on this day. Because Christmas falls during the summer, South Africans also go to the beach or have a Christmas barbecue. Easter Sunday is another important religious holiday when many people attend church and get together with their families.

## A Lot to Celebrate!

| | |
|---|---|
| January 1 | New Year's Day |
| Second Monday in March | Commonwealth Day |
| March/April (dates change from year to year) | Good Friday and Easter |
| March/April (date changes from year to year) | Family Day |
| March 21 | Human Rights Day |
| April 27 | Freedom Day |
| May 1 | Workers Day |
| June 16 | Youth Day |
| August 9 | National Women's Day |
| September 24 | Heritage Day |
| December 16 | Day of Reconciliation |
| December 25 | Christmas |
| December 26 | Day of Goodwill |

Ladysmith Black
Mambazo

# THE ARTS

Arts and crafts have been woven into South African culture for hundreds of years. Ancient people created cave paintings called *rock art*. These rock engravings told stories of African history. South Africans also created statues, pottery, baskets, and beadwork. Many of these traditional arts are still practiced today.

Modern artists have used art to show the injustice of apartheid. The harsh lives in black townships are often the subject of paintings and photographs.

Theater is an important part of South African life. Many plays have **political** themes. South African plays, such as *Sarafina!* and *Master Harold . . . and the Boys*, have been performed in the United States and Europe. These plays showed people around the world what South African culture and life were like.

South Africa is home to many different kinds of music. Traditional instruments include drums, reed pipes, and the *mbira* (a gourd covered with metal strips). Singing is also popular. Afrikaner folk music, or *boeremusiek*, is enjoyed throughout the country. This music features the accordion and sounds a lot like German folk music.

Ladysmith Black Mambazo is an African choir that is well known around the world. This group performs a type of music called *mbube*. Mbube combines Western harmonies and African rhythms.

South Africans living in black townships enjoy jazz music called *marabi* or *mbaqanga*. Meanwhile, most large cities have orchestras and opera companies that perform classical music.

One of South Africa's most famous musicians is Hugh Masekela. Masekela is a black trumpet player who left South Africa in search of greater freedom. In 1968, his song "Grazin' in the Grass" sold millions of copies worldwide. Later, he helped write the musical play *Sarafina!*, which was performed on Broadway. Masekela has also performed with world-famous South African singer Miriam Makeba, who has been called "Mama Africa."

**CAN YOU TELL ME HOW TO GET TO SESAME STREET?**

If you can't, Ladysmith Black Mambazo can. Mambazo's appearance with Paul Simon on *Sesame Street* is among the top three requested segments since the show began. The group also performed on Simon's popular 1986 album *Graceland*.

Tribal dances are a vital part of South African life. South Africa's native people have performed ceremonial dances for hundreds of years. The Zulu tribe is known for its special dances performed at weddings and other important events.

The majority of South African literature is written in English. As with other art forms, political and social issues are popular. *Cry, the Beloved Country* by Alan Paton told the world what was happening in South Africa during the early years of apartheid. Another white writer, Nadine Gordimer, won the Nobel Prize for Literature in 1991. Her short stories and novels about life under apartheid were banned by South Africa's white government for many years. Black writer Athol Fugard's plays show the prejudices between blacks and whites.

**SOUTH AFRICAN DUET**

Both Hugh Masekela and Miriam Makeba have performed their way into South African musical history. For more information on both artists, go to http://africanmusic.org/artists/masekela.html. This site on Masekela has a link to one on Makeba.

During the 1970s, many black poets became famous. Oswald Mtshali, Sipho Sepamla, and Wally Mongane Serote are all respected black South African poets.

# CHAPTER 7

# What's Ahead?

## A Look at South Africa's Future

S outh Africa has a promising outlook. It has a strong economy, many resources, and a beautiful natural environment. However, the country's social and political history has always been a challenge.

## RACIAL EQUALITY

Whites make up only about 17 percent of South Africa's population. However, they still control most of the country's wealth. Almost all the country's high-paying professional jobs are held by whites. However, since the end of apartheid, blacks and coloreds have more opportunities and are starting to enter fields that were once closed to them. In spite of this, most low-paying jobs are still held by people of color.

Schoolchil
in Sow
South A

Education is another area where things are not equal. Although all South African children must go to school, white schools are much better than black schools. Black schools often have few books or supplies, poorly trained teachers, and shabby buildings. It will take a great deal of money to bring the standards of black schools up to the level that white students enjoy. The same is true of housing and other social services. Although all races are now equal under the law, the country still has a long way to go to make that equality a reality.

Basketweaver
from Transvaal,
South Africa

South Africa has taken steps to change the living conditions of its poorest residents. The Reconstruction and Development Program was founded by Nelson Mandela's government after the 1994 elections. It is working to improve the health, education, housing, and working conditions of South Africa's disadvantaged people.

## HEALTH CONCERNS AFFECT ALL

Over four million adults and children living in South Africa suffer from HIV or AIDS. That's one out of every five South Africans. Hundreds die from these diseases every day. These numbers are scary and have forced the country to seek solutions to this health **epidemic**.

The huge number of people infected with HIV and AIDS in South Africa affects many aspects of life there. Hospitals are overcrowded and often don't have enough money for treatments for everyone. Businesses and farming are suffering because so many workers are sick. People must spend so much of their money on treatments that they aren't able to buy other goods. This affects the country's economy. Perhaps most important, families are losing loved ones every day to this terrible disease.

In the past few years, South Africans have begun to realize that HIV and AIDS are not "someone else's problem." Many individuals and groups have tried to provide medical attention and education to their communities. They strive to help those already suffering and prevent further spreading of the disease.

## LOOKING FORWARD

Despite its history of apartheid, violence, and illness, South Africa is one of the most stable and peaceful countries in Africa today. Although it faces many issues, the future looks bright for this country, which is finally coming together after years of division.

Downtown
Cape Town,
South Africa

# INTERNET CONNECTIONS
# TO SOUTH AFRICA

## Just the Facts!

http://www.southafrica-travel.net/
Use this online guide to Africa to learn all about the country.

http://www.geographia.com/south-africa/
This Geographia site features information on South Africa's people, history, geography, and wildlife and includes links to some of South Africa's national parks.

## Chapter 1

http://www.safari-iafrica.com/safari/
Visit the Cape of Good Hope, the Kango Caves of Little Karroo, and other "places to go" in Africa.

http://www.go2africa.com/south-africa/
Tour many of South Africa's beautiful natural features (Table Mountain, Karroo, Drakensberg mountain range, etc.) at this travel site.

## Chapter 2

http://www.wildlifepics.co.za/
Enjoy these spectacular photos of South Africa's wildlife. Then play a game of wildlife memory match.

http://www.raingod.com/angus/Gallery/Photos/Africa/SouthAfrica/index.html
Click on this Web site to view the country's landscapes, birds, and other animals.

## Chapter 3

http://www.museum.co.za/index.htm
Learn about the early French settlers who inhabited the Cape, as well as the Khoikhoi people, at this Western Cape museum site.

http://www.anc.org.za/people/mandela.html
Read more about Nelson Mandela at this African National Congress Web site.

## Chapter 4

http://www.southafrica-travel.net/economy/economy.htm
For quick facts and graphs of information on South Africa's resources, products, mining, and agriculture, visit this site.

## Chapter 4 (cont.)

http://goldinstitute.org/
If the promise of gold sparks your interest, check out this site that's filled with history, facts, and stories about this element.

## Chapter 5

http://www.capetown.gov.za/visitors/default.asp
Click on this official Cape Town tourism and business Web site for information on life in this South African city.

http://www.marques.co.za/clients/zulu
View pictures of beautiful Zulu beadwork and read about the history of these people and their art.

## Chapter 6

http://www.3men.com/south.htm
Learn how to cook a variety of South African dishes at this recipe site.

http://www.mambazo.com/index.html
This is the official Web site of South Africa's award-winning choir, Ladysmith Black Mambazo, whose powerful music is known around the world. Read a biography of the group's musical history, check out the projects they've worked on in the U.S., and even learn some Zulu phrases.

http://www.nobel.se/literature/laureates/1991/gordimer-bio.html
Read a biography of Nadine Gordimer, a respected South African author, at this site.

http://www.iainfisher.com/fugard.html
This fan site is filled with information on South Africa's best-known playwright, Athol Fugard.

## Chapter 7

http://www.mg.co.za
Read South Africa's largest newspaper for articles on current events and issues.

# GLOSSARY

| | |
|---|---|
| **ancestor** | person in a family who came before others |
| **apartheid** | system of laws and government policies that separated the races in South Africa from 1948 to 1994 |
| **biome** | major plant and/or animal community |
| **climate** | usual weather in a place |
| **colony** | place that is ruled by another country |
| **combine** | machine used to harvest grain |
| **conifer** | evergreen tree that produces cones |
| **consumer goods** | products that satisfy human needs and wants |
| **descent** | heritage; coming from a particular place |
| **desert** | area of land that receives very little rain |
| **economy** | a country's system of making, selling, and buying goods and services |
| **epidemic** | large outbreak of a disease |
| **ethnic** | relating to a group of people who share a common race, religion, or culture |
| **executive** | relating to the process of carrying out or enforcing laws |
| **export** | products sold to other countries |
| **hardwood** | having seeds not grown in cones and producing a very solid wood |
| **humid** | having a lot of moisture |
| **irrigation** | process of bringing water to a place by artificial means, such as pipes |
| **judicial** | relating to the process of judging those who break laws |
| **legislative** | relating to the process of making laws |
| **migrating** | moving from one region or climate to another for feeding or breeding |
| **native** | originally living or growing in a certain place |

| | |
|---|---|
| **nomad** | person who moves from place to place in search of food |
| **plateau** | high, flat area of land |
| **political** | relating to government actions, practices, and policies |
| **predator** | animal that hunts other animals for food |
| **prey** | animal that is eaten by another animal |
| **province** | area in a country with strong local governments as well as a central government |
| **rain forest** | thick, tropical forest where a lot of rain falls |
| **rationed** | divided into small shares |
| **republic** | government having elected officials |
| **resource** | material that is valuable or useful |
| **riot** | public fighting, usually involving large groups of people |
| **rural** | having to do with life in the country |
| **savanna** | hot, dry grasslands |
| **scavenger** | animal that eats other animals that are already dead |
| **temperate** | having temperatures that are neither too hot nor too cold |
| **tropical** | having a hot, rainy climate |
| **urban** | having to do with life in the city |
| **Western** | relating to the western region of the world, especially the United States |
| **wicket** | three stumps topped by two crosspieces at which the ball is bowled in cricket |

# INDEX